Sean Kenney

Cool Creations

in

Pieces

Christy Ottaviano Books

Henry Holt and Company

New York

CONTENTS

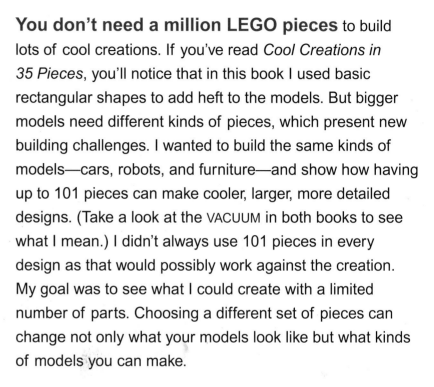

You don't need a million LEGO pieces to build lots of cool creations. If you've read *Cool Creations in 35 Pieces*, you'll notice that in this book I used basic rectangular shapes to add heft to the models. But bigger models need different kinds of pieces, which present new building challenges. I wanted to build the same kinds of models—cars, robots, and furniture—and show how having up to 101 pieces can make cooler, larger, more detailed designs. (Take a look at the VACUUM in both books to see what I mean.) I didn't always use 101 pieces in every design as that would possibly work against the creation. My goal was to see what I could create with a limited number of parts. Choosing a different set of pieces can change not only what your models look like but what kinds of models you can make.

I love how pieces can be combined in unusual ways, stretching the creative possibilities to their limits. Study some of the cutaways to learn how I built the insides of the models, and try using these tricks to make your own crazy contraptions. When you're done, put them online at www.seankenney.com/101 so I can see what you've made with just 101 pieces.

Have fun!

Sean Kenney

Here are the **101 pieces** I've used
throughout the book for each creation.

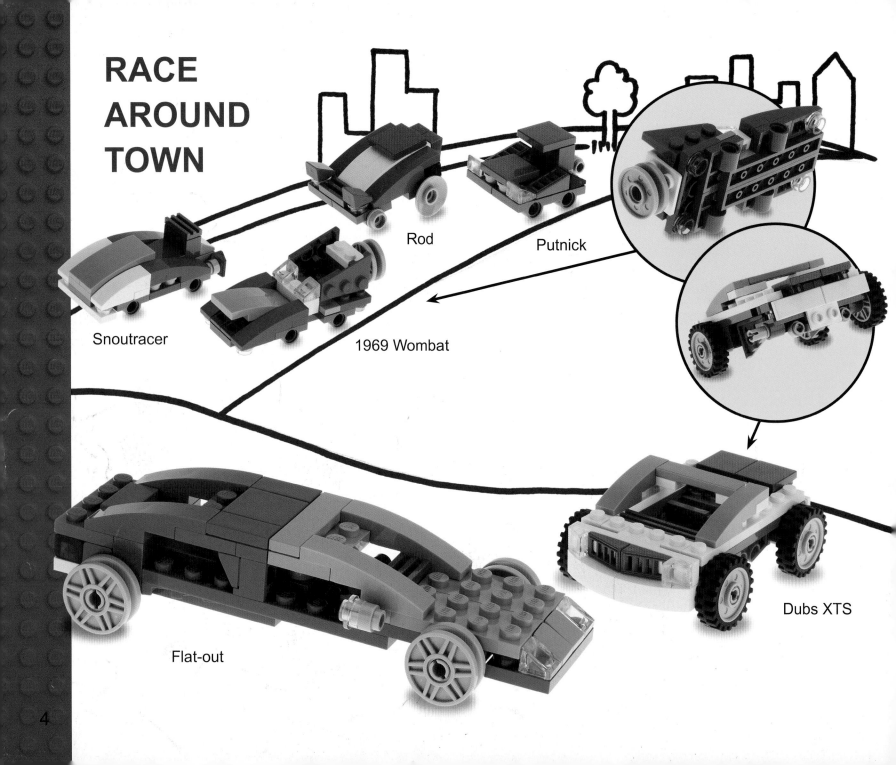

RACE AROUND TOWN

Rod

Putnick

Snoutracer

1969 Wombat

Flat-out

Dubs XTS

Streetslicer

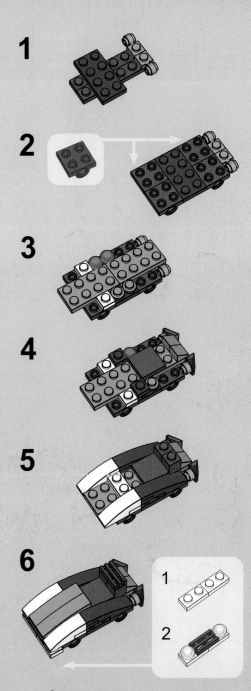

1

2

3

4

5

6

1

2

Snoutracer

THE FINAL STRETCH

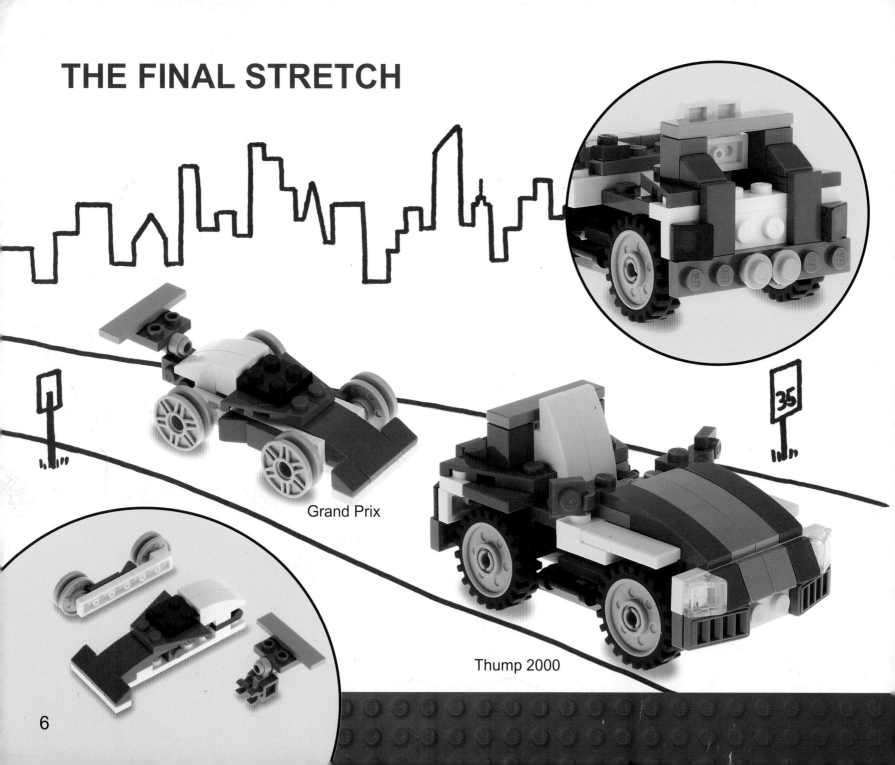

Grand Prix

Thump 2000

35

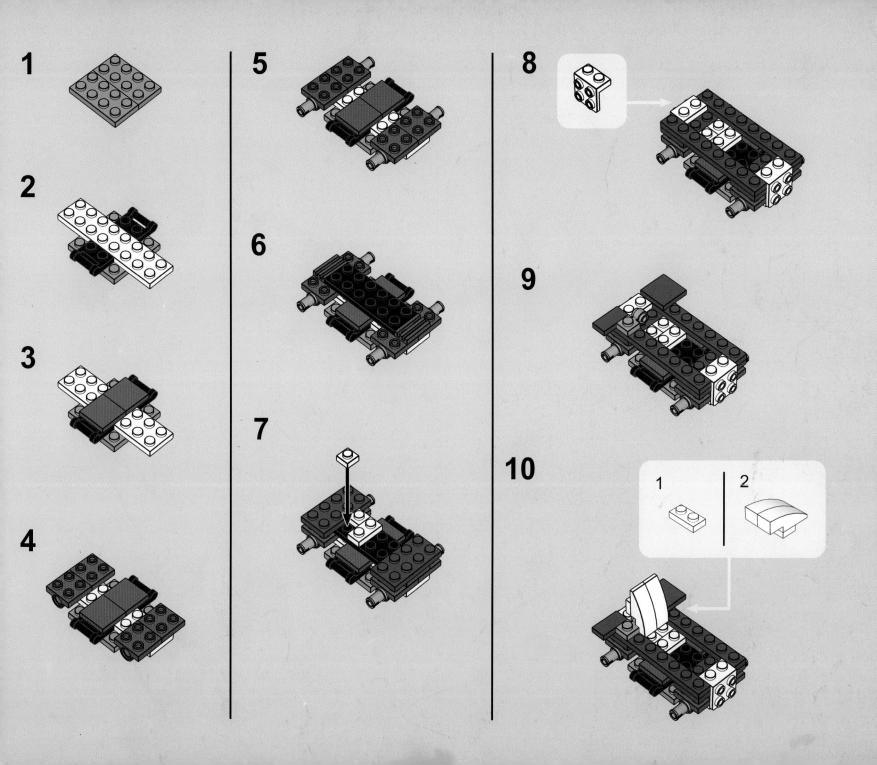

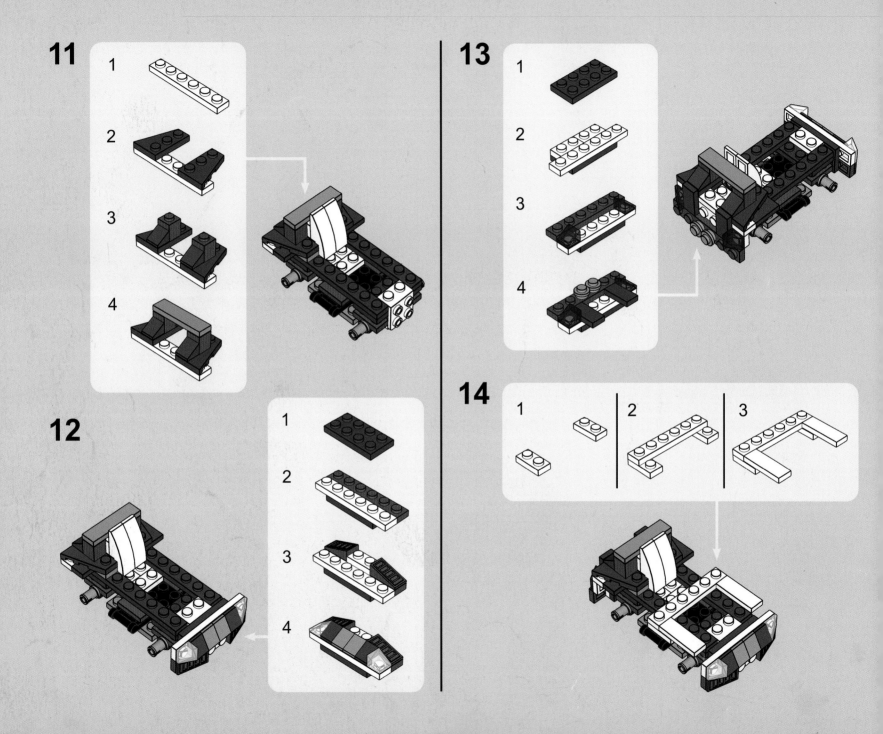

11

1

2

3

4

12

13

1

2

3

4

14

1

2

3

15

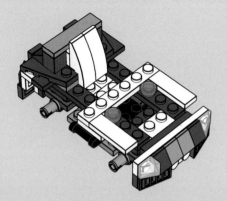

16

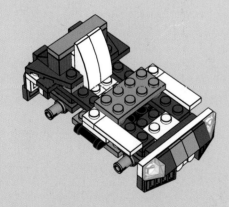

17

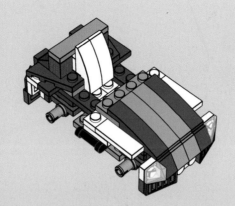

18

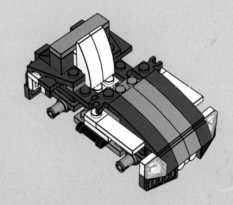

19

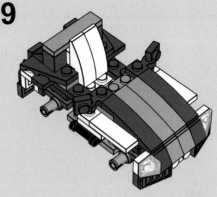

20

x4

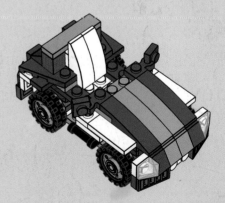

Thump 2000

HARD-WORKING WHEELS

Soapbox Racer

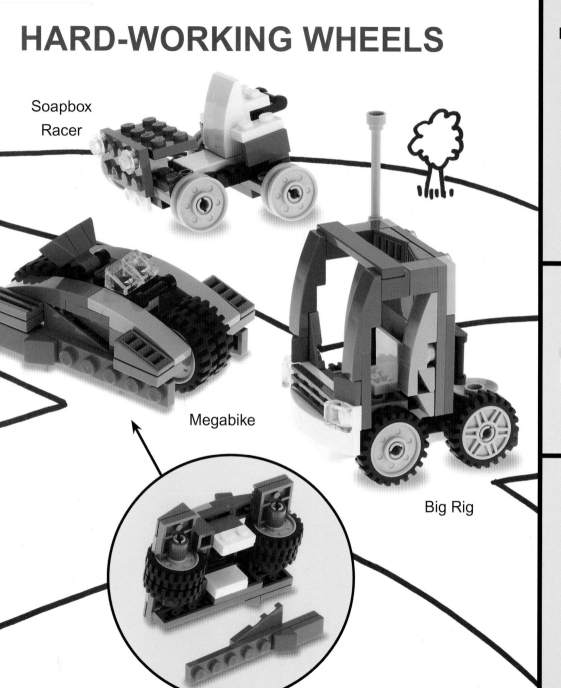

Megabike

Big Rig

Big Rig

Jeep

11

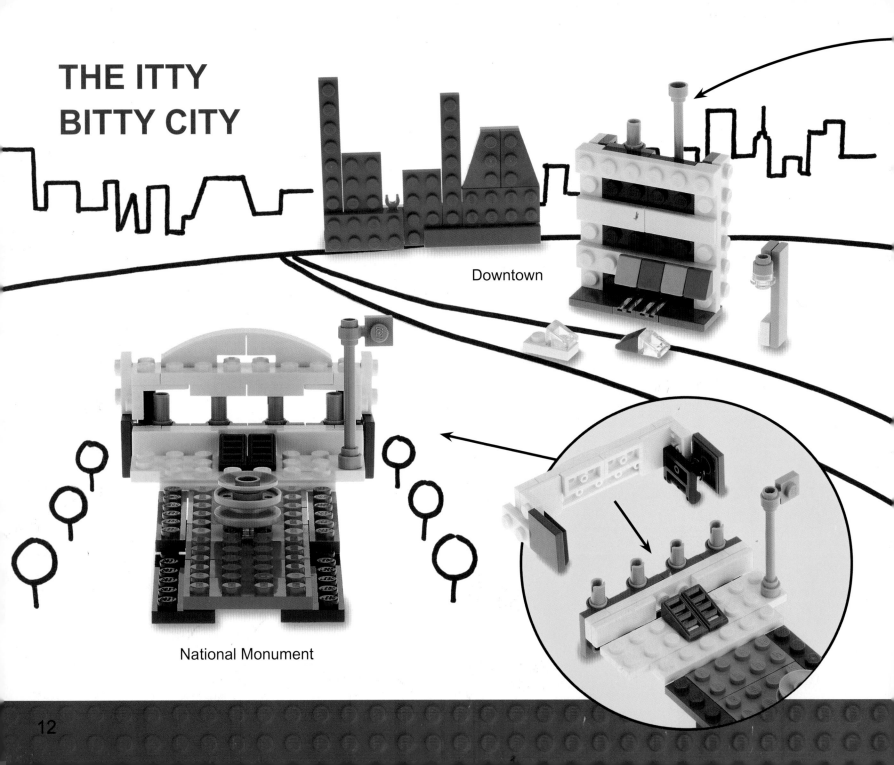

THE ITTY BITTY CITY

Downtown

National Monument

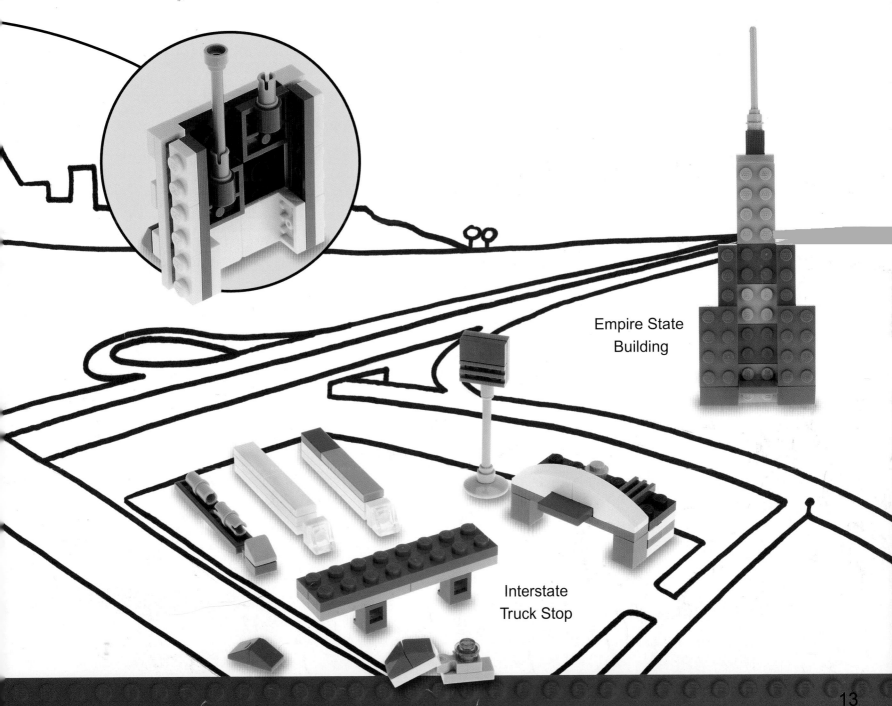

Empire State Building

Interstate Truck Stop

13

1

2

3

4

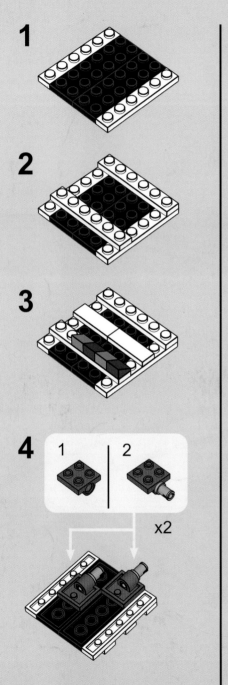

1 | 2

x2

5

1

2

6

1

2

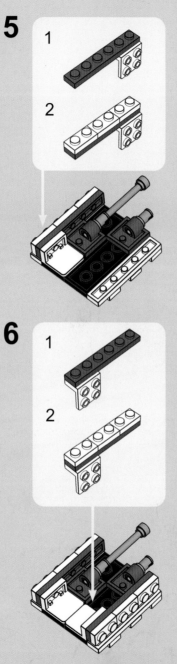

7

1

2

3

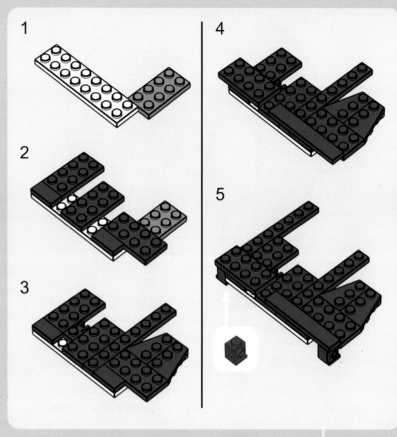

1

2

3

4

5

Downtown

ON THE HIGH SEAS

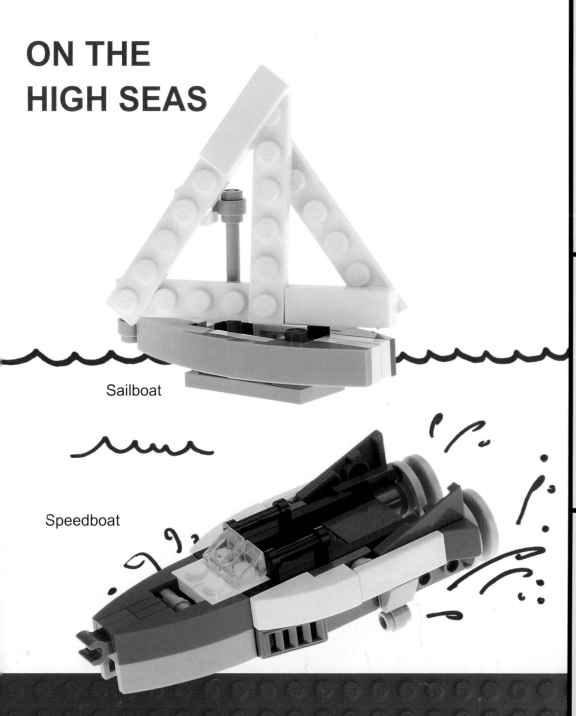

Sailboat

Speedboat

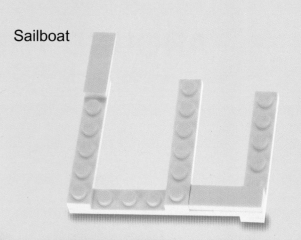

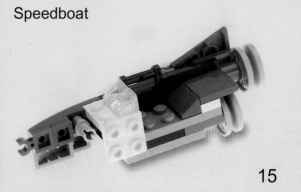

Speedboat

15

AROUND THE HOUSE

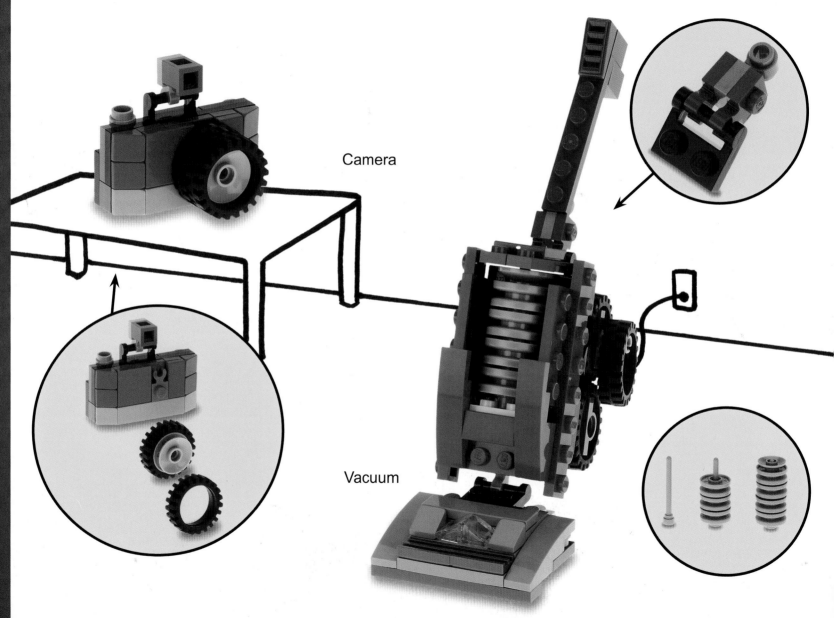

Camera

Vacuum

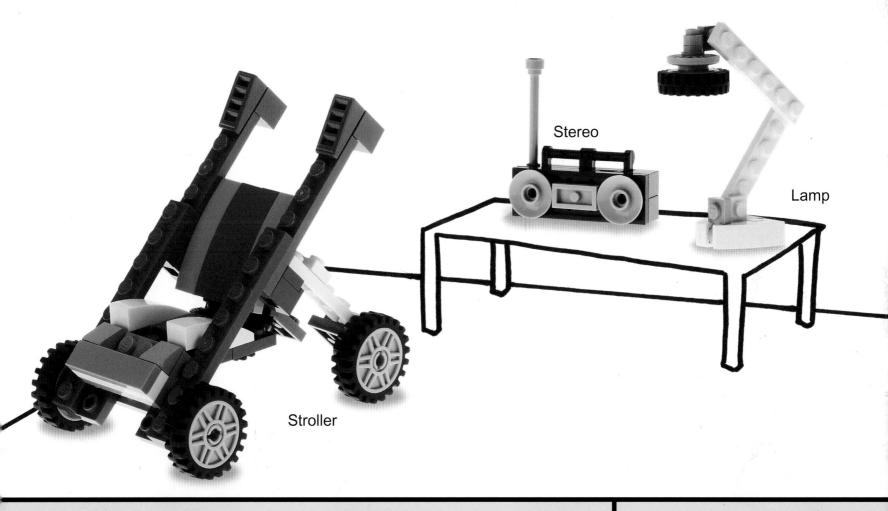

Stroller

Stereo

Lamp

17

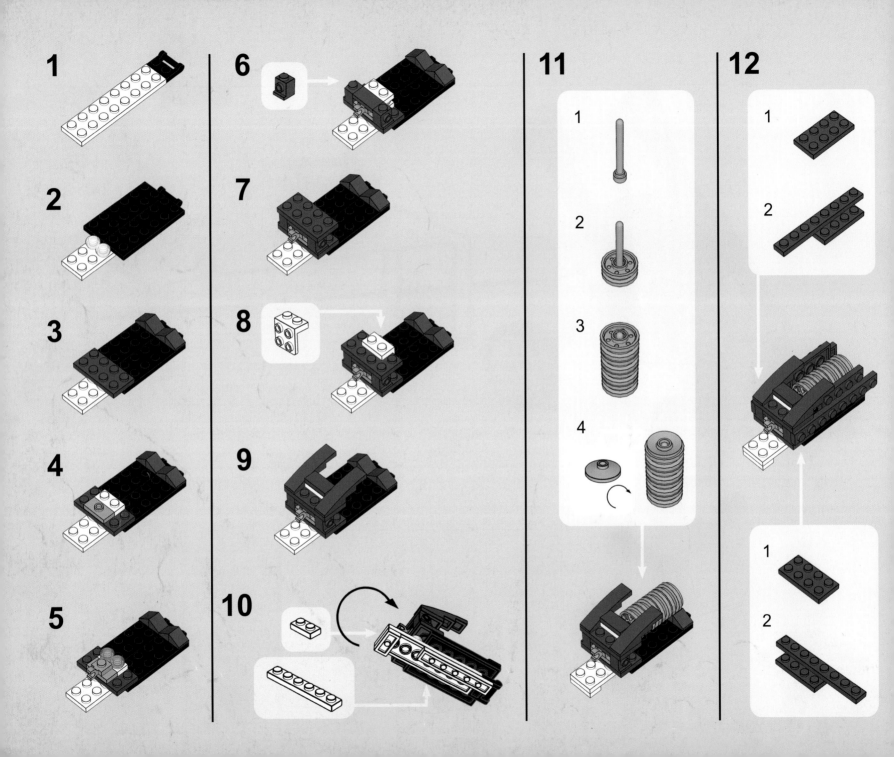

13

1

2

14

1

2

1

2

3

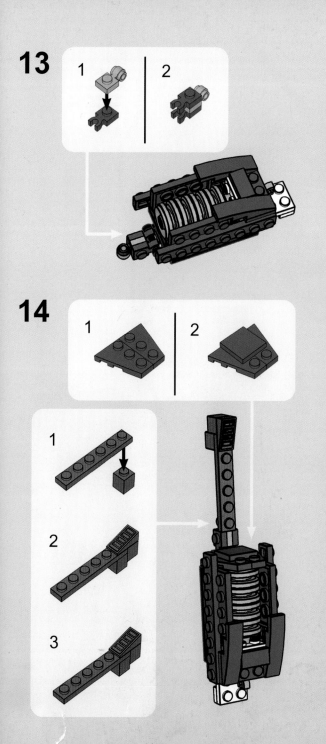

15

1

2

3

x2

4

5

6

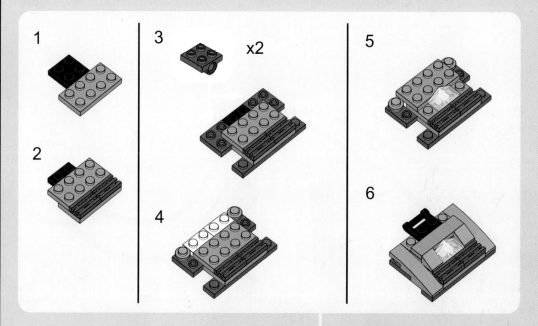

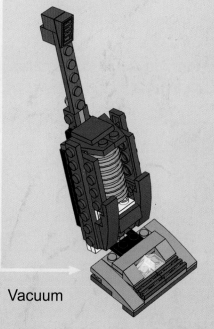

Vacuum

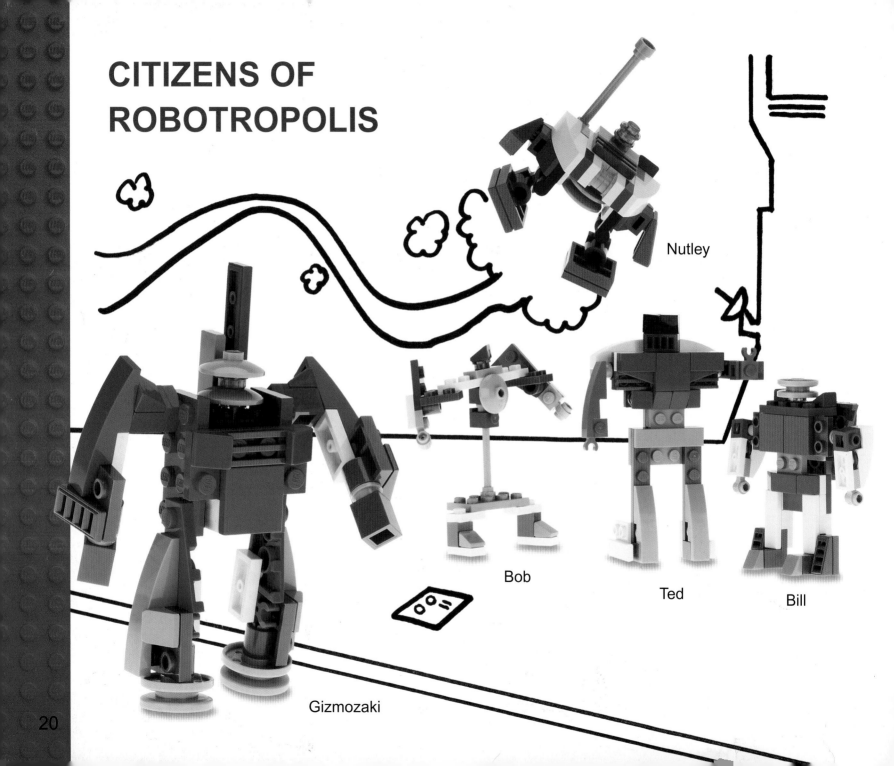

CITIZENS OF ROBOTROPOLIS

Nutley

Gizmozaki

Bob

Ted

Bill

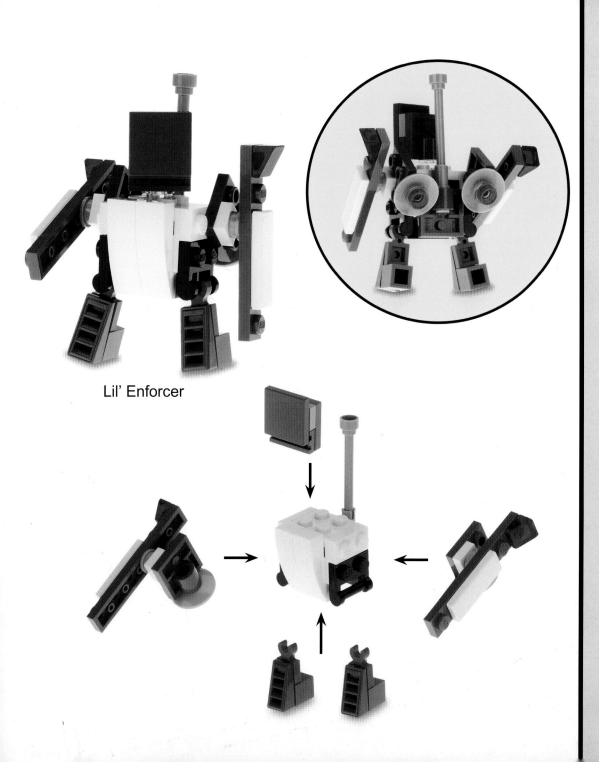

Lil' Enforcer

Lil' Enforcer

Nutley

INTERIOR DECORATING

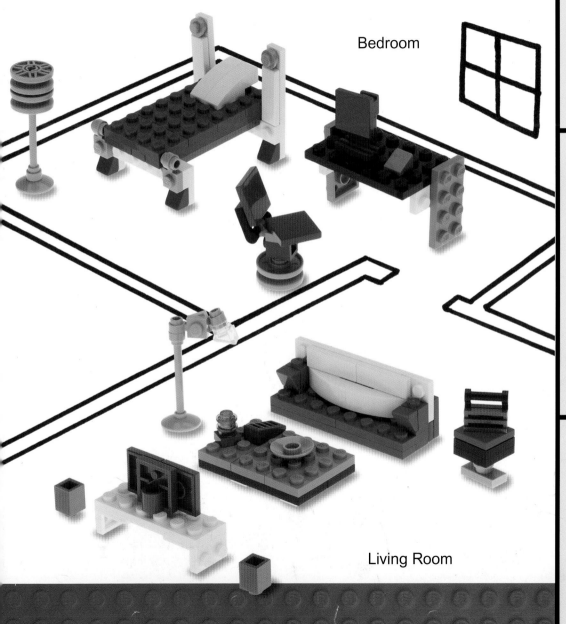

Bedroom

Living Room

Chair

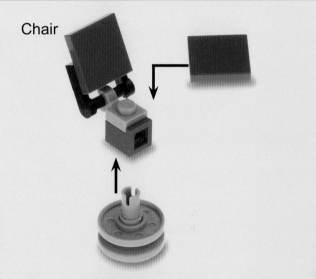

Couch

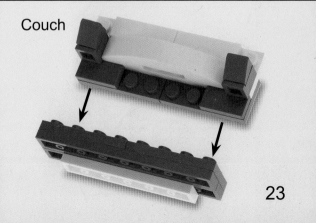

23

ACROSS SPACE

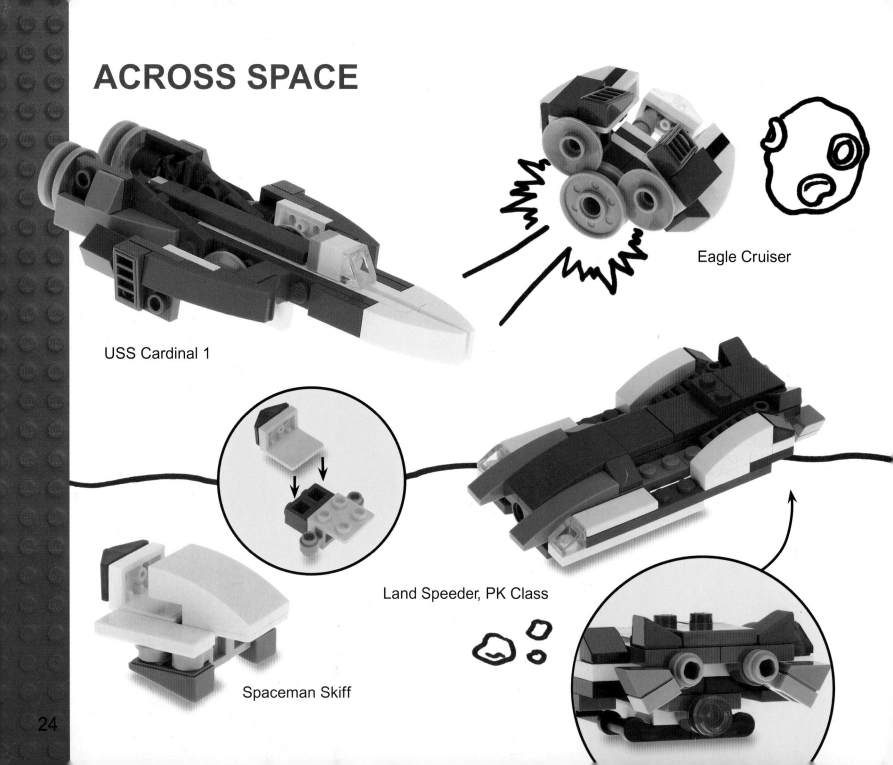

USS Cardinal 1

Eagle Cruiser

Land Speeder, PK Class

Spaceman Skiff

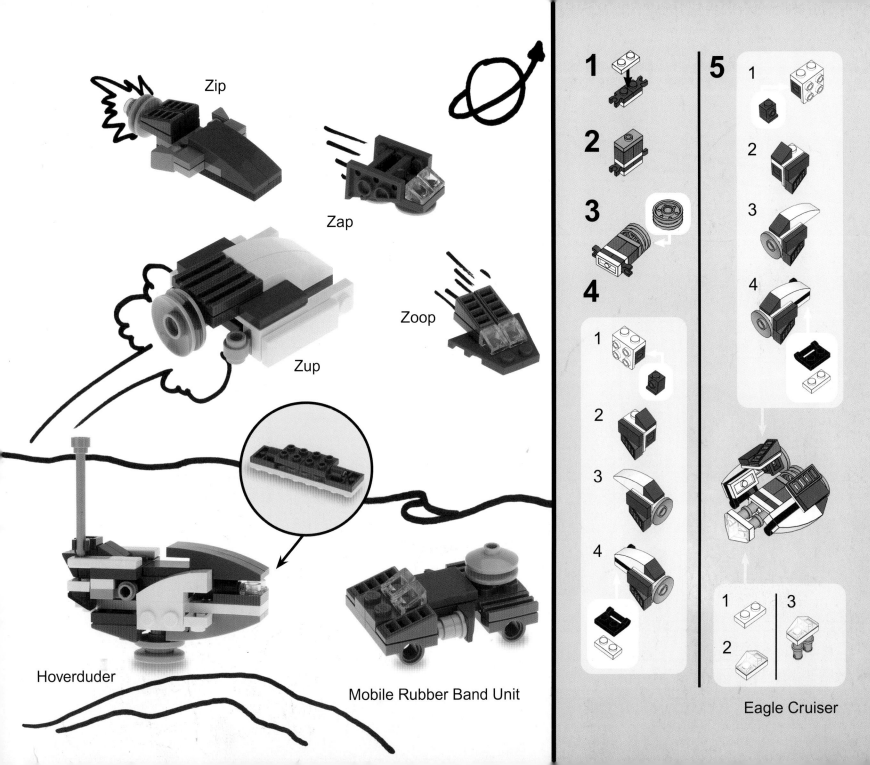

Zip

Zap

Zoop

Zup

Hoverduder

Mobile Rubber Band Unit

1

2

3

4

1

2

3

4

5

1

2

3

4

1

2

3

Eagle Cruiser

GALACTIC DART

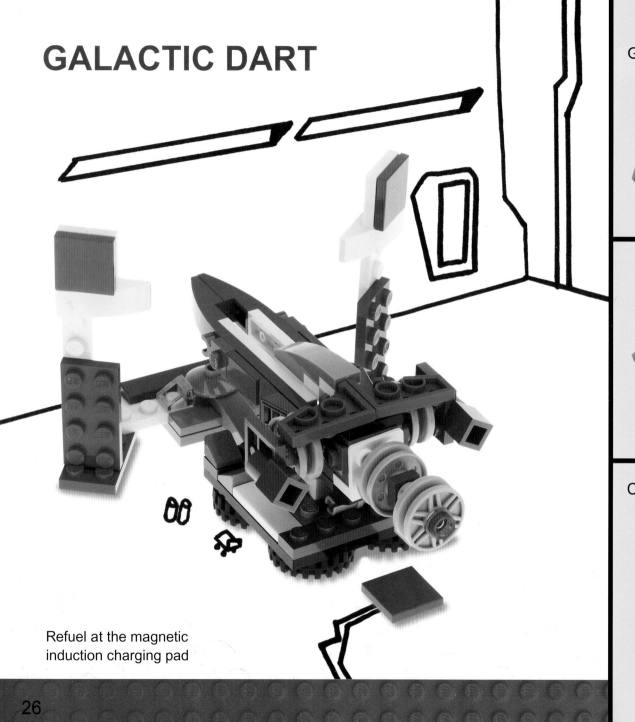

Refuel at the magnetic
induction charging pad

Galactic Dart

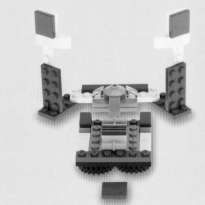

Charging Pad

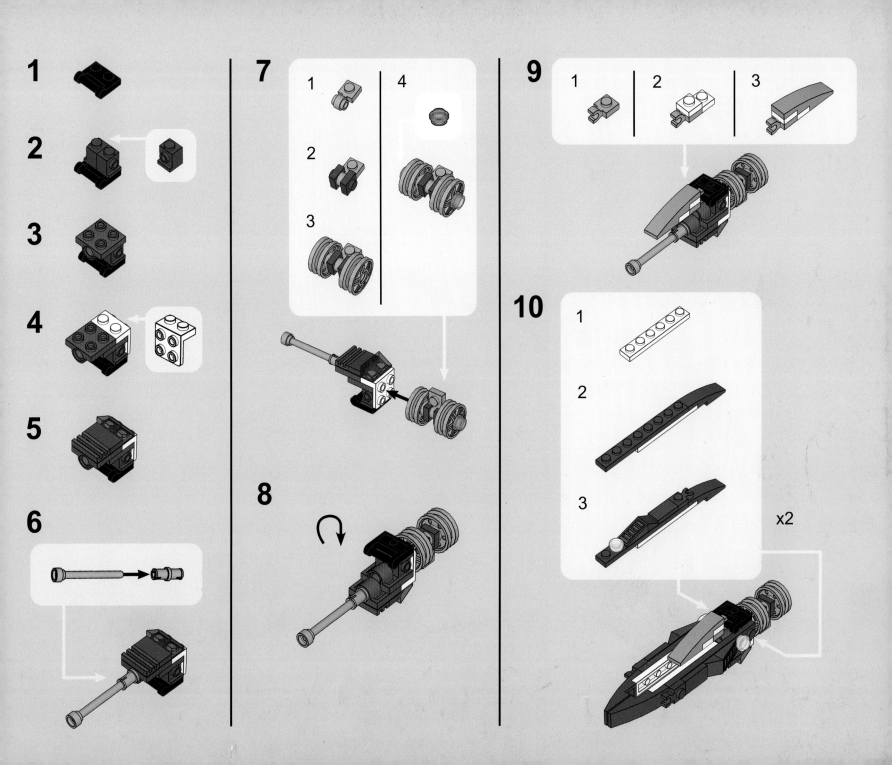

11

1
2

3
4

x2

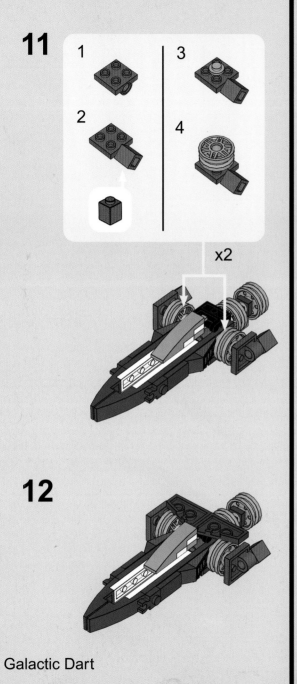

12

Galactic Dart

1

2

3

4

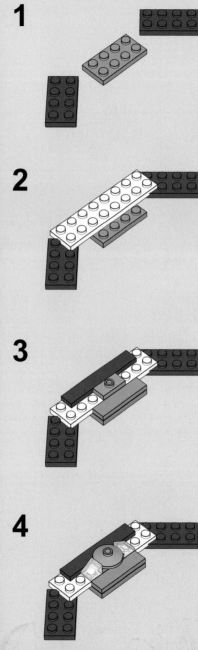

5

1
2
3

1
2
3

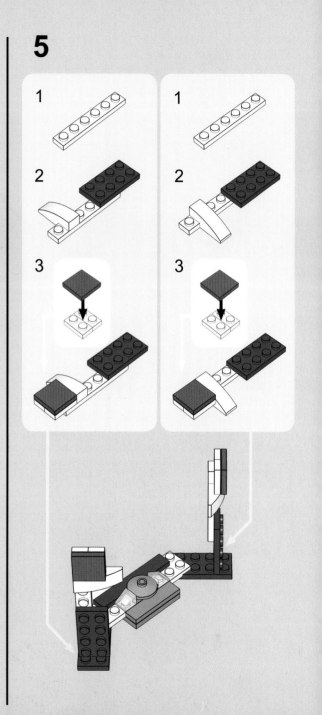

6

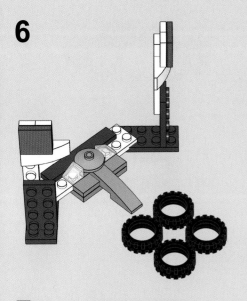

7

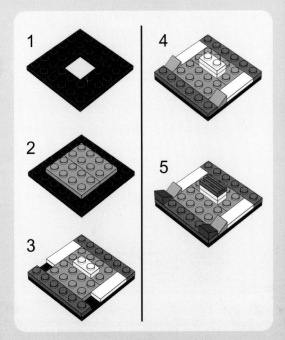

1

2

3

4

5

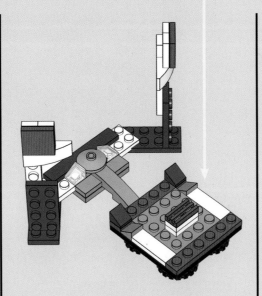

8

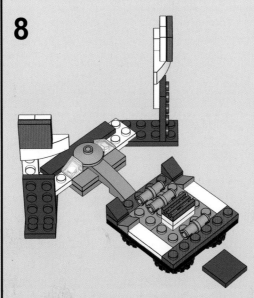

Charging Pad

Land the Galactic Dart on the Charging Pad to refuel!

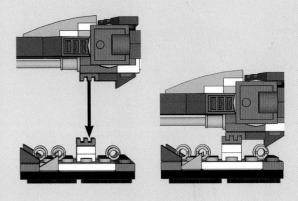

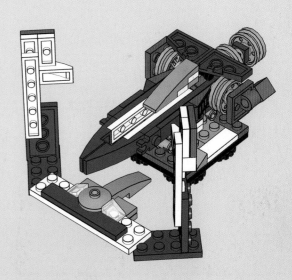

Galactic Dart and Charging Pad

GOOFY FACES

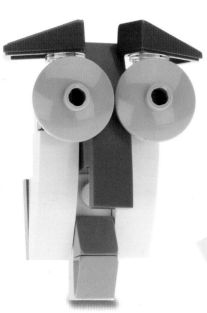

Zapple

Goob

Edgar C. Fethington

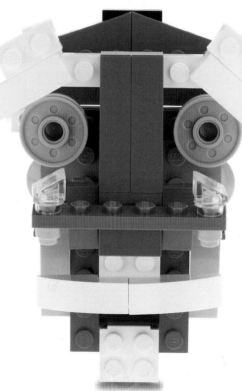

Doc

Master Sensei

Professor
Leopoldi

Submerged
Crocodile

IN THE WILD

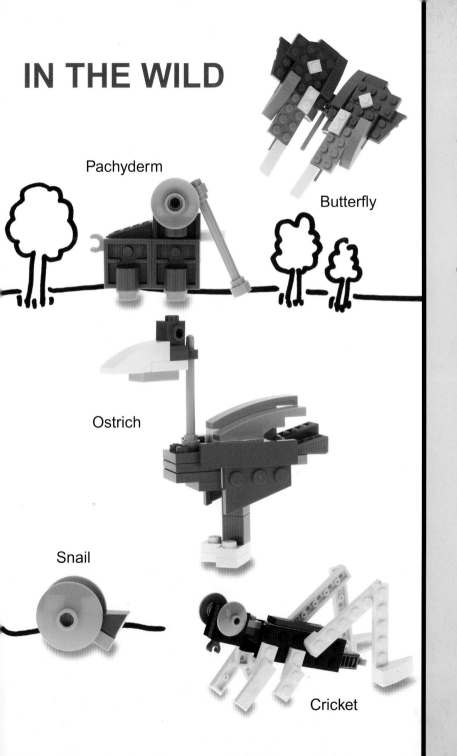

Pachyderm

Butterfly

Ostrich

Snail

Cricket

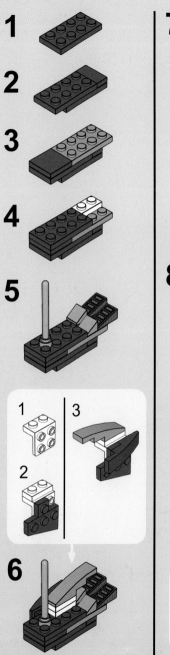

1

2

3

4

5

6

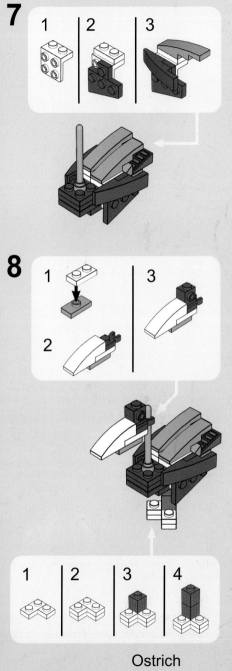

7

| 1 | 2 | 3 |

8

| 1 | 3 |
| 2 | |

| 1 | 2 | 3 | 4 |

Ostrich

For JuJu

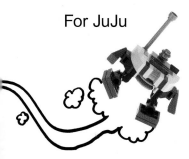

Henry Holt and Company, LLC
Publishers since 1866
175 Fifth Avenue
New York, New York 10010
mackids.com

Henry Holt® is a registered trademark of Henry Holt and Company, LLC.
Copyright © 2014 by Sean Kenney
All rights reserved.

LEGO®, the brick configuration, and the minifigure are trademarks of
The LEGO Group, which does not sponsor, authorize, or endorse this book.

Library of Congress Control Number: 2014932640
ISBN 978-1-62779-017-8

Christy Ottaviano Books/Henry Holt Books for Young Readers may be
purchased for business or promotional use. For information on bulk purchases,
please contact Macmillan Corporate and Premium Sales Department at (800)
221-7945 x5442 or by e-mail at specialmarkets@macmillan.com.

First Edition—2014
LEGO bricks were used to create the models for this book.
The models were photographed by John E. Barrett.
All line drawings were created by Sean Kenney.

Printed in China by Macmillan Production Asia Ltd., Kowloon Bay, Hong Kong
(vendor code: 10)

10 9 8 7 6 5 4 3 2 1

About Sean

Sean Kenney is the creator of *Cool Creations in 35 Pieces*, *Cool Cars and Trucks*, *Cool Robots*, *Cool City*, *Cool Castles*, and *Amazing ABC*. He creates sculptures, models, mosaics, and portraits for venues around the globe. Sean is recognized as one of the premier LEGO brick builders in the world. Visit Sean at seankenney.com.